Financial Success: A Practical Guide

- Introduction to Personal Finance
- Setting Financial Goals
- Creating a Budget
- Reducing Debt
- Building an Emergency Fund
- Investing for the Future
- Maximizing Income
- Saving for Retirement
- Protecting Your Assets with Insurance
- Managing Credit and Credit Scores
- Dealing with Financial Emergencies
- Making Smart Financial Decisions
- Building Long-Term Wealth
- Achieving Financial Freedom
- Maintaining Financial Health

Chapter1: Introduction to Personal Finance

Personal finance is the process of managing your money and making informed financial decisions in order to achieve your financial goals and build long-term financial security. It involves understanding your financial situation, setting financial goals, creating a budget, reducing debt, saving and investing, and making smart financial decisions. Personal finance also involves protecting your assets with insurance and managing credit and credit scores.

In this chapter, we will provide a comprehensive overview of the key concepts and principles of personal finance and how they can be applied to your daily life. We will discuss the importance of setting financial goals, which can help you define your financial priorities and give you a sense of direction and purpose. Setting financial goals can also help you stay motivated and focused on your financial journey.

We will also cover the importance of creating a budget, which is a key tool for managing your finances and staying on track towards your financial goals. A budget allows you to track your income and expenses, identify areas where you can save money, and allocate your resources effectively. We will provide tips and strategies for creating and sticking to a budget, as well as tools and resources that can help you get started.

In addition to setting financial goals and creating a budget, personal finance also involves reducing debt, which can be a major roadblock to financial freedom. We will discuss strategies for paying off debt, including strategies for tackling high-interest debt and strategies for consolidating or refinancing debt. We will also cover the importance of building an emergency fund, which can help you weather financial storms and avoid the need to take on more debt in case of unexpected expenses.

Personal finance also involves saving and investing for the long term. We will discuss the importance of saving for retirement, as well as the various retirement savings options available, such as 401(k)s and IRAs. We will also cover the basics of investing, including the different types of investments available and how to create a diversified investment portfolio.

Finally, we will discuss the importance of making smart financial decisions and protecting your assets with insurance. We will cover the basics of credit and credit scores, and provide tips for managing credit and improving your credit score. We will also discuss the different types of insurance available and how to choose the right coverage for your needs.

Whether you are just starting out or have been managing your finances for years, this chapter will provide a solid foundation for understanding and improving your personal financial situation. We will provide practical tips and tools for making informed financial decisions and staying on track towards your financial goals.

Chapter 2: Setting Financial Goals

Setting financial goals is an essential step in the process of managing your finances and achieving financial success. Financial goals help you define your financial priorities and give you a sense of direction and purpose. They can also help you stay motivated and focused on your financial journey.

In this chapter, we will discuss the importance of setting financial goals and provide tips and strategies for setting and achieving your financial goals. We will cover the different types of financial goals you may want to consider, such as short-term goals, medium-term goals, and long-term goals.

Short-term financial goals are goals that can be achieved within a year or less, such as saving for a down payment on a car or paying off credit card debt. These goals can provide a sense of accomplishment and help you build momentum towards your longer-term goals.

Medium-term financial goals are goals that can be achieved within a few years, such as saving for a down payment on a home or paying off student loans. These goals may require more planning and discipline, but they can help you build a solid foundation for your long-term financial goals.

Long-term financial goals are goals that can take five years or more to achieve, such as saving for retirement or paying for a child's education. These goals may require a more comprehensive financial plan and a long-term perspective, but they can provide a sense of security and stability for the future.

Regardless of the type of financial goals you set, it is important to make them specific, measurable, attainable, relevant, and time-bound (SMART). SMART goals are specific, meaning they are clear and defined. They are measurable, meaning you can track your progress towards achieving them. They are attainable, meaning they are realistic and achievable given your current resources and circumstances. They are relevant, meaning they are aligned with your values and priorities. And they are time-bound, meaning they have a specific deadline or timeframe. SMART goals can help you make your goals more achievable and increase your chances of success.

In addition to setting financial goals, it is also important to create a financial plan to help you track your progress and make adjustments as needed. A financial plan is a detailed roadmap for achieving your financial goals. It should include your income, expenses, and assets, as well as a budget and a plan for saving and investing. A financial plan can help you identify potential roadblocks and make adjustments as needed to stay on track towards your financial goals.

We will provide tips and strategies for creating a financial plan and resources that can help you get started. Whether you are just starting out or have been managing your finances for a while, this chapter will provide valuable insights and practical tools for setting and achieving your financial goals. By setting and working towards financial goals, you can take control of your finances and build a solid foundation for long-term financial success.

Chapter 3: Creating a Budget

A budget is a key tool for managing your finances and staying on track towards your financial goals. A budget allows you to track your income and expenses, identify areas where you can save money, and allocate your resources effectively. It can also help you avoid overspending and debt, and provide a sense of control over your finances.

In this chapter, we will discuss the importance of creating a budget and provide tips and strategies for creating and sticking to a budget. We will cover the different types of budgets you can use, such as a zero-based budget, a 50/30/20 budget, and a cash budget. We will also discuss the importance of tracking your expenses and adjusting your budget as needed.

To create a budget, you will need to gather information about your income and expenses. Your income includes any money you receive from sources such as your job, investments, or other sources. Your expenses include any money you spend on things such as housing, food, transportation, and entertainment. You will need to track your income and expenses for a period of time, such as a month, to get a clear picture of your financial situation.

Once you have gathered this information, you can create a budget by setting aside money for your fixed expenses, such as rent or mortgage payments, and allocating the rest of your money to your variable expenses, such as food, transportation, and entertainment. You can also set aside money for savings and investments, such as an emergency fund or a retirement account.

It is important to track your expenses and compare them to your budget to ensure you are staying on track. If you find that you are overspending in certain areas, you may need to make adjustments to your budget to bring your spending in line with your income. You can also use budgeting tools and apps to help you track your expenses and stay on track with your budget.

By creating and sticking to a budget, you can take control of your finances and make progress towards your financial goals. We will provide tips and strategies for creating and sticking to a budget, as well as resources that can help you get started. Whether you are just starting out or have been managing your finances for a while, this chapter will provide valuable insights and practical tools for creating and maintaining a budget.

Chapter 4: Reducing Debt

Debt can be a major roadblock to financial freedom and stability. It can also be a source of stress and anxiety, and can impact your credit score and financial future. Reducing debt is an important step in the process of managing your finances and achieving financial success.

In this chapter, we will discuss the importance of reducing debt and provide tips and strategies for paying off debt. We will cover the different types of debt, including secured debt (debt that is secured by collateral, such as a mortgage or car loan) and unsecured debt (debt that is not secured by collateral, such as credit card debt). We will also discuss the importance of prioritizing your debt, and strategies for tackling high-interest debt and consolidating or refinancing debt.

One common strategy for paying off debt is the debt snowball method, which involves focusing on paying off your smallest debt first and then working your way up to your larger debts. This method can help you build momentum and motivation as you see your debts being paid off one by one. Another common strategy is the debt avalanche method, which involves focusing on paying off your highest-interest debt first to save money on interest in the long run.

It is important to create a budget and allocate a portion of your income towards paying off debt. You may also want to consider cutting expenses, increasing your income, or using debt consolidation or refinancing to help you pay off your debts more quickly.

In addition to paying off debt, it is also important to build an emergency fund to help you weather financial storms and avoid the need to take on more debt in case of unexpected expenses. An emergency fund is a savings account set aside for unexpected expenses, such as medical bills or car repairs. It is generally recommended to have enough money in your emergency fund to cover three to six months' worth of expenses.

By reducing debt and building an emergency fund, you can take control of your finances and make progress towards your financial goals. We will provide tips and strategies for paying off debt and building an emergency fund, as well as resources that can help you get started. Whether you are just starting out or have been managing your finances for a while, this chapter will provide valuable insights and practical tools for reducing debt and building financial stability.

It is important to create a budget and allocate a portion of your income towards paying off debt. You may also want to consider cutting expenses, increasing your income, or using debt consolidation or refinancing to help you pay off your debts more quickly.

In addition to paying off debt, it is also important to build an emergency fund to help you weather financial storms and avoid the need to take on more debt in case of unexpected expenses. An emergency fund is a savings account set aside for unexpected expenses, such as medical bills or car repairs. It is generally recommended to have enough money in your emergency fund to cover three to six months' worth of expenses.

By reducing debt and building an emergency fund, you can take control of your finances and make progress towards your financial goals. We will provide tips and strategies for paying off debt and building an emergency fund, as well as resources that can help you get started. Whether you are just starting out or have been managing your finances for a while, this chapter will provide valuable insights and practical tools for reducing debt and building financial stability.

Chapter 5: Building an Emergency Fund

An emergency fund is a savings account set aside for unexpected expenses, such as medical bills or car repairs. It is generally recommended to have enough money in your emergency fund to cover three to six months' worth of expenses. An emergency fund can provide a financial cushion in case of unexpected expenses and can help you avoid the need to take on more debt.

In this chapter, we will discuss the importance of building an emergency fund and provide tips and strategies for building and maintaining an emergency fund. We will cover the different types of emergency fund options, such as a high-yield savings account or a money market account, and how to choose the right option for your needs. We will also discuss the importance of building an emergency fund as part of a broader financial plan and how to balance the need for an emergency fund with other financial goals, such as saving for retirement or paying off debt.

To build an emergency fund, you will need to set aside a portion of your income on a regular basis. You may want to start small and gradually increase the amount you save over time. You may also want to consider automating your savings by setting up automatic transfers from your checking account to your emergency fund.

It is important to keep your emergency fund separate from your other savings and to only use it for true emergencies. This can help you avoid the temptation to dip

A high-yield savings account is a type of savings account that offers a higher interest rate than a traditional savings account. These accounts are FDIC-insured, which means that your money is backed by the Federal Deposit Insurance Corporation (FDIC) up to $250,000 per depositor. High-yield savings accounts can be a good option for an emergency fund because they offer a higher interest rate than a traditional savings account, which can help your money grow faster.

A money market account is a type of savings account that offers a higher interest rate than a traditional savings account and may also offer check-writing and debit card privileges. Money market accounts are FDIC-insured up to $250,000 per depositor. Money market accounts can be a good option for an emergency fund because they offer a higher interest rate than a traditional

It is important to build an emergency fund as part of a broader financial plan and to balance the need for an emergency fund with other financial goals, such as saving for retirement or paying off debt. By building an emergency fund and having a plan in place for unexpected expenses, you can increase your financial stability and reduce your risk of financial emergencies. We will provide tips and strategies for building and maintaining an emergency fund, as well as resources that can help you get started. Whether you are just starting out or have been managing your finances for a while, this chapter will provide valuable insights and practical tools for building an emergency fund and increasing your financial stability.

Chapter 6: Investing for the Future

Investing is an important step in the process of managing your finances and achieving financial success. Investing can help you grow your wealth over time, diversify your portfolio, and prepare for the future.

In this chapter, we will discuss the importance of investing and provide tips and strategies for investing for the long term. We will cover the different types of investments, such as stocks, bonds, mutual funds, and exchange-traded funds (ETFs), and how to choose the right investments for your goals and risk tolerance. We will also discuss the importance of developing a diversified investment portfolio and the role of asset allocation in investing.

To invest for the long term, you will need to set financial goals and determine your risk tolerance. Your financial goals should be specific, measurable, attainable, relevant, and time-bound (SMART). Your risk tolerance is the level of risk you are willing and able to take on in your investments. It is important to consider your risk tolerance when choosing investments, as higher-risk investments can offer higher potential returns but also come with a higher level of risk.

Once you have set your financial goals and determined your risk tolerance, you can choose investments that align with your goals and risk tolerance. There are several types of investments you can consider, including stocks, bonds, mutual funds, and ETFs. Stocks are a type of investment that represents ownership in a company. They offer the potential for capital appreciation, but also come with the risk of loss. Bonds are a type of investment that represents a loan to a company or government. They offer the potential for income and stability, but also come with the risk of default. Mutual funds are a type of investment that pools money from many investors

Bonds are a type of investment that represents a loan to a company or government. When you buy a bond, you are lending money to the issuer in exchange for interest payments and the return of principal at maturity. Bonds offer the potential for income and stability, as they generally have a fixed interest rate and a fixed maturity date. However, bonds also come with the risk of default, or the inability of the issuer to make the required interest and principal payments. Mutual funds are a type of investment that pools money from many investors and uses it to buy a diversified portfolio of stocks, bonds, or other securities. Mutual funds offer the benefits of diversification and professional management, but also come with fees, such as expense ratios and sales charges.

Exchange-traded funds (ETFs) are a type of investment that tracks the performance of a particular market index, such as the S&P 500. ETFs offer the benefits of diversification and low costs, but also come with the risk of market fluctuations.

It is important to develop a diversified investment portfolio, which means having a mix of different types of investments to reduce risk and increase the potential for returns. Asset allocation is the process of dividing your investments among different asset classes, such as stocks, bonds, and cash, to create a balanced portfolio that aligns with your financial goals and risk tolerance.

To invest for the long term, you will need to set financial goals and determine your risk tolerance. Your financial goals should be specific, measurable, attainable, relevant, and time-bound (SMART). Your risk tolerance is the level of risk you are willing and able to take on in your investments. It is important to consider your risk tolerance when choosing investments, as higher-risk investments can offer higher potential returns but also come with a higher level

Chapter 7: Maximizing Income

Maximizing income is an important step in the process of managing your finances and achieving financial success. Increasing your income can help you build wealth, pay off debt, and achieve your financial goals.

In this chapter, we will discuss the importance of maximizing income and provide tips and strategies for increasing your income. We will cover the different ways to increase your income, such as asking for a raise, negotiating your salary, starting a side hustle, or investing in yourself through education or training. We will also discuss the importance of setting income goals and tracking your progress towards achieving those goals.

To increase your income, you will need to identify your strengths and skills and look for ways to leverage them. You may want to consider asking for a raise or negotiating your salary at your current job, or you may want to explore new job opportunities that offer higher pay. You may also want to consider starting a side hustle, or a part-time business or gig that can provide additional income.

Investing in yourself through education or training can also help you increase your income. By learning new skills or obtaining a higher level of education, you may be able to qualify for higher-paying jobs or advance in your career.

It is important to set income goals and track your progress towards achieving those goals. Setting income goals can help you stay motivated and focused on increasing your income. Tracking your progress can help you identify areas for improvement and measure your success.

By maximizing your income and setting income goals, you can take control of your finances and make progress towards your financial goals. We will provide tips and strategies for increasing your income, as well as resources that can help you get started. Whether you are just starting out or have been managing your finances for a while, this chapter will provide valuable insights and practical tools for maximizing your income and achieving financial success.

Asking for a raise or negotiating your salary at your current job can be an effective way to increase your income. To ask for a raise, you will want to do your research, prepare a compelling case, and practice your presentation. You can research the going rate for your position in your industry and location, and consider factors such as your job performance, contributions to the company, and any additional responsibilities you have taken on. You can prepare a compelling case by highlighting your accomplishments, demonstrating your value to the company, and explaining why you deserve a raise. You can practice your presentation by rehearsing your arguments, anticipating questions, and being confident and assertive.

Chapter 8: Saving for Retirement

Saving for retirement is an important step in the process of managing your finances and achieving financial success. Saving for retirement can help you build a secure financial future and ensure that you have enough money to live on during your retirement years.

In this chapter, we will discuss the importance of saving for retirement and provide tips and strategies for saving for retirement. We will cover the different types of retirement savings accounts, such as a 401(k) or an IRA, and how to choose the right accounts for your needs. We will also discuss the role of Social Security in retirement planning and the importance of developing a retirement plan.

There are several types of retirement savings accounts that you can consider, such as a 401(k), an IRA, or a taxable investment account. A 401(k) is a type of employer-sponsored retirement savings plan that allows you to contribute a portion of your income on a tax-deferred basis. An IRA is an individual retirement account that allows you to save for retirement on a tax-advantaged basis. A taxable investment account is a type of investment account that is not tax-advantaged, but can still be used to save for retirement.

To choose the right retirement savings accounts for your needs, you will want to consider factors such as the contribution limits, tax benefits, fees, and investment options. You should also consider whether you are eligible to contribute to a 401(k) or an IRA, and whether you have the ability to contribute to multiple accounts.

Social Security is a federal program that provides a source of income for retirees, disabled individuals, and survivors. Social Security is funded through payroll taxes and is designed to provide a basic level of income for retirees. However, it is important to note that Social Security benefits are generally not enough to sustain a comfortable retirement on their own, and it is generally recommended to save for retirement in addition to receiving Social Security benefits.

Developing a retirement plan can help you stay on track and achieve your retirement goals. A retirement plan should include a detailed budget, a savings plan, and an investment strategy. It is important to review your retirement plan regularly and make adjustments as needed.

By saving for retirement and developing a retirement plan, you can build a secure financial future and ensure that you have enough money to

Chapter 9: Protecting Your Assets with Insurance

Insurance is an important tool for protecting your assets and managing risk. Insurance can help you protect against financial loss due to unexpected events, such as accidents, natural disasters, or medical emergencies.

In this chapter, we will discuss the importance of insurance and provide tips and strategies for choosing the right insurance coverage. We will cover the different types of insurance, such as life, health, home, and auto insurance, and how to choose the right coverage for your needs. We will also discuss the importance of reviewing and updating your insurance coverage on a regular basis.

There are several types of insurance that you may want to consider, such as life insurance, health insurance, home insurance, and auto insurance. Life insurance is a type of insurance that provides financial protection to your loved ones in the event of your death. Health insurance is a type of insurance that helps cover the cost of medical care, including hospital stays, doctor visits, and prescription medications. Home insurance is a type of insurance that helps protect your home and possessions from damage or loss due to unexpected events, such as fires, natural disasters, or burglaries. Auto insurance is a type of insurance that helps protect you and your vehicle from financial loss due to accidents or other incidents.

To choose the right insurance coverage, you will want to consider factors such as your needs, your budget, and the available options. You should also consider the reputation and financial stability of the insurance company, as well as the terms and conditions of the policy.

It is important to review and update your insurance coverage on a regular basis, as your needs and circumstances may change over time. You should review your insurance coverage at least once a year to ensure that it still meets your needs and that you are getting the best value for your money. You should also update your insurance coverage when you experience significant life events, such as getting married, having a child, or buying a new home.

By protecting your assets with insurance and reviewing and updating your coverage on a regular basis, you can increase your financial stability and peace of mind. We will provide tips and strategies for choosing the right insurance coverage, as well as resources that can help you get started. Whether you are just starting out or have been managing your finances for a while, this chapter will provide valuable insights and practical tools for protecting your assets with insurance.

Chapter 10: Managing Credit and Credit Scores

Credit and credit scores are important factors in managing your finances and achieving financial success. Credit refers to the ability to borrow money, and a credit score is a numerical representation of your creditworthiness. Credit scores are used by lenders to assess your risk as a borrower and to determine whether to extend credit to you and at what terms.

In this chapter, we will discuss the importance of managing credit and credit scores and provide tips and strategies for improving your credit. We will cover the different types of credit, such as revolving credit and installment credit, and how to use credit responsibly. We will also discuss the importance of monitoring your credit and correcting any errors on your credit reports.

There are two main types of credit: revolving credit and installment credit. Revolving credit is a type of credit that allows you to borrow up to a certain limit and pay back the balance over time, such as a credit card. Installment credit is a type of credit that requires you to make fixed payments over a set period of time, such as a mortgage or a car loan.

To use credit responsibly, you will want to pay your bills on time, keep your balances low, and use a diverse mix of credit. You should also be mindful of your credit utilization ratio, which is the amount of credit you are using compared to your credit limit. A high credit utilization ratio can have a negative impact on your credit score.

It is important to monitor your credit and correct any errors on your credit reports. You can request a free copy of your credit report from each of the three major credit bureaus (Experian, Equifax, and TransUnion) once a year. You should review your credit reports for accuracy and report any errors to the credit bureaus. You can also monitor your credit scores to track your progress and identify areas for improvement.

By managing your credit and credit scores, you can increase your financial stability and access to credit. We will provide tips and strategies for improving your credit, as well as resources that can help you get started. Whether you are just starting out or have been managing your finances for a while, this chapter will provide valuable insights and practical tools for managing credit and credit scores.

Chapter 11: Dealing with Financial Emergencies

Financial emergencies can be stressful and disruptive, and it is important to have a plan in place to deal with them. A financial emergency is a unexpected event that requires immediate financial attention, such as a medical emergency, a natural disaster, or the loss of a job.

In this chapter, we will discuss the importance of preparing for financial emergencies and provide tips and strategies for dealing with them. We will cover the different types of financial emergencies, such as medical emergencies, natural disasters, and job loss, and how to prepare for them. We will also discuss the role of emergency savings and insurance in helping you cope with financial emergencies.

To prepare for financial emergencies, you will want to create an emergency savings fund, review your insurance coverage, and develop a financial emergency plan. An emergency savings fund is a set amount of money set aside specifically for emergencies. It is generally recommended to save at least three to six months' worth of expenses in an emergency savings fund. You should review your insurance coverage to ensure that you have adequate protection for different types of emergencies, such as medical emergencies, natural disasters, or job loss. You should also develop a financial emergency plan that outlines what you will do in the event of an emergency, such as how you will pay for unexpected expenses, how you will communicate with your loved ones, and how you will access your emergency savings.

When dealing with a financial emergency, it is important to stay calm and take decisive action. You should prioritize your expenses and focus on meeting your basic needs, such as food, shelter, and medical care. You should also communicate with your loved ones and seek support from friends, family, or community resources. You should also consider using your emergency savings or insurance to cover the costs of the emergency, if appropriate.

By preparing for financial emergencies and having a plan in place to deal with them, you can increase your financial stability and resilience. We will provide tips and strategies for preparing for financial emergencies, as well as resources that can help you get started. Whether you are just starting out or have been managing your finances for a while, this chapter will provide valuable insights and practical tools for dealing with financial emergencies.

Chapter 12: Making Smart Financial Decisions

Making smart financial decisions is an important part of managing your finances and achieving financial success. Financial decisions involve choosing how to allocate your financial resources, such as your money, time, and energy, in a way that aligns with your goals and values.

In this chapter, we will discuss the importance of making smart financial decisions and provide tips and strategies for making better financial choices. We will cover the different types of financial decisions, such as spending, saving, investing, and borrowing, and how to make informed and well-informed decisions in each area. We will also discuss the role of financial planning and goal setting in helping you make smart financial decisions.

To make smart financial decisions, you will want to consider your goals, your values, and your resources. You should also consider the risks and rewards of different financial options, as well as the pros and cons of each choice. You should also be aware of your biases and limitations, and seek out additional information and advice as needed.

Financial planning is the process of organizing and managing your financial resources in a way that helps you achieve your goals. Financial planning involves setting financial goals, creating a budget, and making a plan for how to allocate your resources. Goal setting is an important part of financial planning, as it helps you identify what you want to achieve and how you will get there. A budget is a tool that helps you track your income and expenses and make informed financial decisions.

By making smart financial decisions and engaging in financial planning and goal setting, you can increase your financial stability and achieve your financial goals. We will provide tips and strategies for making better financial choices, as well as resources that can help you get started. Whether you are just starting out or have been managing your finances for a while, this chapter will provide valuable insights and practical tools for making smart financial decisions.

- Consider your goals, values, and resources when making financial decisions
- Evaluate the risks and rewards of different financial options
- Be aware of your biases and limitations, and seek out additional information and advice as needed
- Engage in financial planning and goal setting to help you make informed financial decisions
- Use tools such as budgets to track your income and expenses and make informed financial decisions

Chapter 13: Building Long-Term Wealth

Building long-term wealth is an important part of achieving financial success and security. Long-term wealth is the accumulation of financial assets over an extended period of time, with the goal of providing financial stability and independence in the future.

In this chapter, we will discuss the importance of building long-term wealth and provide tips and strategies for accumulating financial assets over the long term. We will cover the different types of financial assets, such as stocks, bonds, real estate, and businesses, and how to choose the right mix of assets for your goals and risk tolerance. We will also discuss the role of diversification, compound interest, and patience in building long-term wealth.

To build long-term wealth, you will want to choose a mix of financial assets that aligns with your goals and risk tolerance. You should also consider the importance of diversification, which is the practice of spreading your investments across different asset classes and sectors to reduce risk. Compound interest is the interest that is earned on the original principal and on the accumulated interest of an investment over time. By investing early and allowing compound interest to work for you, you can significantly increase your long-term wealth.

Patience is also a key factor in building long-term wealth. Building wealth takes time, and it is important to have a long-term perspective and to be patient with your investments. It is also important to review your investments periodically and make adjustments as needed to ensure that they are aligned with your goals and risk tolerance.

By building long-term wealth and engaging in diversification, compound interest, and patience, you can increase your financial stability and achieve your financial goals. We will provide tips and strategies for accumulating financial assets over the long term, as well as resources that can help you get started. Whether you are just starting out or have been managing your finances for a while, this chapter will provide valuable insights and practical tools for building long-term wealth

- Choose a mix of financial assets that aligns with your goals and risk tolerance
- Diversify your investments across different asset classes and sectors to reduce risk
- Take advantage of compound interest by investing early and allowing it to work for you
- Be patient and have a long-term perspective with your investments
- Review your investments periodically and make adjustments as needed to ensure that they are aligned with your goals and risk tolerance

.

Chapter 14: Achieving Financial Freedom

Financial freedom is the ability to have control over your finances and the ability to make choices that align with your values and goals. Financial freedom is achieved through a combination of financial stability, financial independence, and financial security.

In this chapter, we will discuss the importance of achieving financial freedom and provide tips and strategies for achieving financial stability, independence, and security. We will cover the different factors that contribute to financial freedom, such as debt management, budgeting, investing, and saving, and how to incorporate these factors into your financial plan. We will also discuss the role of financial education and professional help in achieving financial freedom.

To achieve financial freedom, you will want to focus on financial stability, independence, and security. Financial stability is the ability to meet your financial obligations and have a sufficient financial cushion to weather financial emergencies. Financial independence is the ability to generate sufficient income to meet your needs without relying on others. Financial security is the ability to have a stable financial future and to be prepared for the unexpected.

To achieve financial stability, you will want to focus on debt management, budgeting, and saving. Debt management involves reducing and eliminating debt, and budgeting involves tracking your income and expenses and making informed financial decisions. Saving is the process of setting aside money for the future, and it is an important part of achieving financial stability.

To achieve financial independence, you will want to focus on earning and investing. Earning involves increasing your income through employment, entrepreneurship, or other means. Investing involves using your money to generate additional income or growth, such as through stocks, bonds, real estate, or businesses.

To achieve financial security, you will want to focus on preparing for the unexpected. This may involve having an emergency savings fund, reviewing your insurance coverage, and developing a financial emergency plan. It may also involve saving for retirement and other long-term goals.

By achieving financial freedom and focusing on financial stability, independence, and security, you can increase your financial control and make choices that align with your values and goals. We will provide tips and strategies for achieving financial freedom, as well as resources

- Achieve financial stability by focusing on debt management, budgeting, and saving
- Achieve financial independence by focusing on earning and investing
- Achieve financial security by preparing for the unexpected, such as through an emergency savings fund and insurance coverage
- Save for retirement and other long-term goals to ensure financial security
- Seek financial education and professional help to increase your financial knowledge and skills and improve your financial planning

Chapter 15: Maintaining Financial Health

Maintaining financial health is an ongoing process that involves regularly reviewing and managing your finances to ensure that you are on track to meet your goals and stay financially stable. Financial health is the ability to manage your finances effectively and to make informed financial decisions that align with your values and goals.

In this chapter, we will discuss the importance of maintaining financial health and provide tips and strategies for maintaining financial stability, independence, and security. We will cover the different factors that contribute to financial health, such as budgeting, saving, investing, and debt management, and how to incorporate these factors into your financial plan. We will also discuss the role of financial education and professional help in maintaining financial health.

To maintain financial health, you will want to regularly review and manage your finances. This may involve creating and maintaining a budget, saving money, investing for the future, and managing your debt. It is also important to periodically review your financial goals and make adjustments as needed to ensure that you are on track to achieve them.

Financial education and professional help can be valuable resources in maintaining financial health. Financial education can help you increase your financial knowledge and skills and make better financial decisions. Professional help, such as a financial advisor or a credit counselor, can provide guidance and support in managing your finances and achieving your financial goals.

By maintaining financial health and focusing on financial stability, independence, and security, you can increase your financial control and make choices that align with your values and goals. We will provide tips and strategies for maintaining financial health, as well as resources that can help you get started. Whether you are just starting out or have been managing your finances for a while, this chapter will provide valuable insights and practical tools for maintaining financial health.

- Review and manage your finances regularly, including creating and maintaining a budget, saving money, investing for the future, and managing your debt
- Periodically review your financial goals and make adjustments as needed
- Seek financial education to increase your financial knowledge and skills
- Seek professional help, such as from a financial advisor or credit counselor, for guidance and support in managing your finances
- Focus on financial stability, independence, and security to maintain financial control and make choices that align with your values and goals

"Achieving financial freedom requires a combination of financial stability, independence, and security. By making smart financial decisions, building long-term wealth, and maintaining financial health, you can increase your financial control and achieve your financial goals."

Author:Sudesh Kumar

www.ingramcontent.com/pod-product-compliance
Lightning Source LLC
LaVergne TN
LVHW020535160826
845677LV00015B/4075

* 9 7 9 8 3 7 0 8 3 4 8 2 0 *